RETIREMENT
WISHES
BUCKET

Copyright © 2021

RETIREMENT
WISHES
BUCKET

THIS BOOK BELONGS TO

_____

_____

« RETIREMENT iS DOING WHAT YOU HAVE FUN DOING »

HOW TO USE THIS BOOK:

This book is a journal to help you create your retirement bucket list. Our retirement years are a perfect opportunity to pursue those dreams that we have always wanted to fulfil; and that we never had time to do. From that, place that you always wanted to visit, to that experience that you have not had yet. Writing down your bucket list is a great way to track your hopes and dreams. This journal is your companion to do that and to track your experience and note your feelings, as it is a future self-journaling tool where you record ideas for items you might include on your bucket list. Whenever you decide to do one of the listed ideas, you can return to this journal and fill in the details and what you did feel.

Here are some Fun Activities, Cute Date Ideas & Romantic Things to take in consideration as inspiration

- **Adopt/rescue a shelter pet,**
- **Fly in a helicopter,**
- **Get a Couples Massage,**
- **Grow a little garden,**
- **Stargaze on a Rooftop,**
- **Learn a foreign language,**
- **Go horseback riding**
- **Donate blood**
- **Hot air balloon ride**
- **Have a Picnic**
- **Volunteer**
- **Play Mini Golf**
- **Climb to the Top of a Mountain**
- **Take A Spontaneous Road Trip**
- **Learn to Tango**
- **Go Wine Tasting**
- **.....**

You can get creative and plan some fun activities and experience some great moments. ENJOY IT.

MY BUCKET LIST

DONE

\# —— ———————————————————— ♡

\# —— ———————————————————— ♡

\# —— ———————————————————— ♡

\# —— ———————————————————— ♡

\# —— ———————————————————— ♡

\# —— ———————————————————— ♡

\# —— ———————————————————— ♡

\# —— ———————————————————— ♡

\# —— ———————————————————— ♡

\# —— ———————————————————— ♡

\# —— ———————————————————— ♡

\# —— ———————————————————— ♡

\# —— ———————————————————— ♡

\# —— ———————————————————— ♡

\# —— ———————————————————— ♡

\# —— ———————————————————— ♡

\# —— ———————————————————— ♡

\# —— ———————————————————— ♡

MY BUCKET LIST

DONE

\# —— _____ ♡

\# —— _____ ♡

\# —— _____ ♡

\# —— _____ ♡

\# —— _____ ♡

\# —— _____ ♡

\# —— _____ ♡

\# —— _____ ♡

\# —— _____ ♡

\# —— _____ ♡

\# —— _____ ♡

\# —— _____ ♡

\# —— _____ ♡

\# —— _____ ♡

\# —— _____ ♡

\# —— _____ ♡

\# —— _____ ♡

\# —— _____ ♡

MY BUCKET LIST

DONE

\# —— _____ ♡

\# —— _____ ♡

\# —— _____ ♡

\# —— _____ ♡

\# —— _____ ♡

\# —— _____ ♡

\# —— _____ ♡

\# —— _____ ♡

\# —— _____ ♡

\# —— _____ ♡

\# —— _____ ♡

\# —— _____ ♡

\# —— _____ ♡

\# —— _____ ♡

\# —— _____ ♡

\# —— _____ ♡

\# —— _____ ♡

\# —— _____ ♡

MY BUCKET LIST

DONE

——— ———————————————————— ♡

——— ———————————————————— ♡

——— ———————————————————— ♡

——— ———————————————————— ♡

——— ———————————————————— ♡

——— ———————————————————— ♡

——— ———————————————————— ♡

——— ———————————————————— ♡

——— ———————————————————— ♡

——— ———————————————————— ♡

——— ———————————————————— ♡

——— ———————————————————— ♡

——— ———————————————————— ♡

——— ———————————————————— ♡

——— ———————————————————— ♡

——— ———————————————————— ♡

——— ———————————————————— ♡

——— ———————————————————— ♡

MY BUCKET LIST

#01

_____

_____

WHO/WHAT INSPIRED ME? _____

I NEED THIS BECAUSE? _____

_____

TO DO THIS I NEED? _____

_____

I DID IT

DATE COMPLETED _____

LOCATION _____

DETAILS _____

_____

_____

_____

_____

WHAT I LEARNED _____

_____

_____

BEST PART _____

_____

_____

WOULD DO IT AGAIN?   YES   NO

MY BUCKET LIST

#02

_____

_____

WHO/WHAT INSPIRED ME? _____

I NEED THIS BECAUSE? _____
_____

TO DO THIS I NEED? _____
_____

I DID IT

DATE COMPLETED _____
LOCATION _____
DETAILS _____
_____
_____
_____
_____

WHAT I LEARNED _____
_____
_____
_____

BEST PART _____
_____
_____

WOULD DO IT AGAIN?   YES ♡   NO ♡

MY BUCKET LIST

#03

_____

_____

WHO/WHAT INSPIRED ME? _____

I NEED THIS BECAUSE? _____

_____

TO DO THIS I NEED? _____

_____

I DID IT

DATE COMPLETED _____

LOCATION _____

DETAILS _____

_____

_____

_____

_____

WHAT I LEARNED _____

_____

_____

BEST PART _____

_____

_____

WOULD DO IT AGAIN? YES ♡   NO ♡

MY BUCKET LIST

#04

_____
_____

WHO/WHAT INSPIRED ME? _____

NEED THIS BECAUSE? _____

O DO THIS I NEED? _____

I DID IT

ATE COMPLETED _____
OCATION _____
ETAILS _____
_____
_____
_____
_____

HAT I LEARNED _____
_____
_____
_____

EST PART _____
_____
_____

WOULD DO IT AGAIN?   YES   NO

MY BUCKET LIST

#05

_____

_____

WHO/WHAT INSPIRED ME? _____

I NEED THIS BECAUSE? _____

_____

TO DO THIS I NEED? _____

_____

I DID IT

DATE COMPLETED _____

LOCATION _____

DETAILS _____

_____

_____

_____

_____

WHAT I LEARNED _____

_____

_____

BEST PART _____

_____

_____

WOULD DO IT AGAIN?   YES ♡   NO ♡

MY BUCKET LIST

#06

_____
_____

WHO/WHAT INSPIRED ME? _____

NEED THIS BECAUSE? _____
_____

O DO THIS I NEED? _____
_____

I DID IT

ATE COMPLETED _____
OCATION _____
ETAILS _____
_____
_____
_____
_____

'HAT I LEARNED _____
_____
_____
_____

EST PART _____
_____
_____

WOULD DO IT AGAIN?   YES   NO

MY BUCKET LIST

#07

_____

_____

WHO/WHAT INSPIRED ME? _____

I NEED THIS BECAUSE? _____

_____

TO DO THIS I NEED? _____

_____

I DID IT

DATE COMPLETED _____

LOCATION _____

DETAILS _____

_____

_____

_____

_____

WHAT I LEARNED _____

_____

_____

BEST PART _____

_____

_____

WOULD DO IT AGAIN?   YES   NO

MY BUCKET LIST

#08

_____

_____

WHO/WHAT INSPIRED ME? _____

I NEED THIS BECAUSE? _____

_____

TO DO THIS I NEED? _____

_____

I DID IT

DATE COMPLETED _____

LOCATION _____

DETAILS _____

_____

_____

_____

WHAT I LEARNED _____

_____

_____

BEST PART _____

_____

_____

WOULD DO IT AGAIN? YES NO

MY BUCKET LIST

#09

_____

_____

WHO/WHAT INSPIRED ME? _____

I NEED THIS BECAUSE? _____

_____

TO DO THIS I NEED? _____

_____

I DID IT

DATE COMPLETED _____

LOCATION _____

DETAILS _____

_____

_____

_____

_____

WHAT I LEARNED _____

_____

_____

BEST PART _____

_____

_____

WOULD DO IT AGAIN? YES   NO

MY BUCKET LIST

#10

_____

_____

WHO/WHAT INSPIRED ME? _____

NEED THIS BECAUSE? _____

O DO THIS I NEED? _____

_____

I DID IT

ATE COMPLETED _____
OCATION _____
ETAILS _____

_____

_____

_____

WHAT I LEARNED _____

_____

_____

EST PART _____

_____

_____

WOULD DO IT AGAIN? YES ♡ NO ♡

MY BUCKET LIST

#11

_____
_____

WHO/WHAT INSPIRED ME? _____

I NEED THIS BECAUSE? _____
_____

TO DO THIS I NEED? _____
_____

I DID IT

DATE COMPLETED _____
LOCATION _____
DETAILS _____
_____
_____
_____
_____

WHAT I LEARNED _____
_____
_____

BEST PART _____
_____
_____

WOULD DO IT AGAIN?   YES ♡   NO ♡

MY BUCKET LIST

#12

WHO/WHAT INSPIRED ME? _____

NEED THIS BECAUSE? _____

TO DO THIS I NEED? _____

I DID IT

DATE COMPLETED _____
LOCATION _____
DETAILS _____

_____
_____
_____
_____

WHAT I LEARNED _____

_____
_____
_____

BEST PART _____

_____
_____

WOULD DO IT AGAIN? YES NO

MY BUCKET LIST

#13

_____

_____

WHO/WHAT INSPIRED ME? _____

I NEED THIS BECAUSE? _____
_____

TO DO THIS I NEED? _____
_____

I DID IT

DATE COMPLETED _____
LOCATION _____
DETAILS _____
_____
_____
_____
_____

WHAT I LEARNED _____
_____
_____

BEST PART _____
_____
_____

WOULD DO IT AGAIN?   YES   NO

MY BUCKET LIST

#14

_____

_____

WHO/WHAT INSPIRED ME? _____

I NEED THIS BECAUSE? _____

TO DO THIS I NEED? _____

I DID IT

DATE COMPLETED _____

LOCATION _____

DETAILS _____

_____

_____

_____

_____

WHAT I LEARNED _____

_____

_____

_____

BEST PART _____

_____

_____

WOULD DO IT AGAIN?   YES   NO

MY BUCKET LIST

#15

_____

_____

WHO/WHAT INSPIRED ME? _____

I NEED THIS BECAUSE? _____

_____

TO DO THIS I NEED? _____

_____

I DID IT

DATE COMPLETED _____

LOCATION _____

DETAILS _____

_____

_____

_____

_____

WHAT I LEARNED _____

_____

_____

BEST PART _____

_____

_____

WOULD DO IT AGAIN?   YES ♡   NO ♡

MY BUCKET LIST

#16

_____

_____

WHO/WHAT INSPIRED ME? _____

NEED THIS BECAUSE? _____
_____

TO DO THIS I NEED? _____
_____

I DID IT

DATE COMPLETED _____
LOCATION _____
DETAILS _____
_____
_____
_____
_____

WHAT I LEARNED _____
_____
_____

BEST PART _____
_____
_____

WOULD DO IT AGAIN?   YES   NO

MY BUCKET LIST

#17

_____
_____

WHO/WHAT INSPIRED ME? _____

I NEED THIS BECAUSE? _____
_____

TO DO THIS I NEED? _____
_____

I DID IT

DATE COMPLETED _____
LOCATION _____
DETAILS _____
_____
_____
_____
_____

WHAT I LEARNED _____
_____
_____

BEST PART _____
_____
_____

WOULD DO IT AGAIN?   YES ♡   NO ♡

MY BUCKET LIST

#18

_____

_____

/HO/WHAT INSPIRED ME? _____

NEED THIS BECAUSE? _____
_____

O DO THIS I NEED? _____
_____

I DID IT

ATE COMPLETED _____

OCATION _____

ETAILS _____
_____
_____
_____
_____

/HAT I LEARNED _____
_____
_____
_____

EST PART _____
_____
_____

NOULD DO IT AGAIN?   YES   NO

MY BUCKET LIST

#19

_____

_____

WHO/WHAT INSPIRED ME? _____

I NEED THIS BECAUSE? _____

_____

TO DO THIS I NEED? _____

_____

I DID IT

DATE COMPLETED _____
LOCATION _____
DETAILS _____

_____

_____

_____

_____

WHAT I LEARNED _____

_____

_____

BEST PART _____

_____

_____

WOULD DO IT AGAIN? YES   NO

MY BUCKET LIST

#20

_____

_____

WHO/WHAT INSPIRED ME? _____

I NEED THIS BECAUSE? _____

_____

TO DO THIS I NEED? _____

_____

I DID IT

DATE COMPLETED _____

LOCATION _____

DETAILS _____

_____

_____

_____

_____

WHAT I LEARNED _____

_____

_____

_____

BEST PART _____

_____

_____

WOULD DO IT AGAIN? YES NO

MY BUCKET LIST

#21

_____

_____

WHO/WHAT INSPIRED ME? _____

I NEED THIS BECAUSE? _____

_____

TO DO THIS I NEED? _____

_____

I DID IT

DATE COMPLETED _____

LOCATION _____

DETAILS _____

_____

_____

_____

_____

WHAT I LEARNED _____

_____

_____

_____

BEST PART _____

_____

_____

WOULD DO IT AGAIN?   YES   NO

MY BUCKET LIST

_____

#22

_____

WHO/WHAT INSPIRED ME? _____

NEED THIS BECAUSE? _____

_____

O DO THIS I NEED? _____

_____

I DID IT

ATE COMPLETED _____

OCATION _____

ETAILS _____

_____

_____

_____

_____

WHAT I LEARNED _____

_____

_____

_____

EST PART _____

_____

_____

WOULD DO IT AGAIN?   YES   NO

MY BUCKET LIST

#23

_____

_____

WHO/WHAT INSPIRED ME? _____

I NEED THIS BECAUSE? _____

_____

TO DO THIS I NEED? _____

_____

I DID IT

DATE COMPLETED _____

LOCATION _____

DETAILS _____

_____

_____

_____

_____

WHAT I LEARNED _____

_____

_____

_____

BEST PART _____

_____

_____

WOULD DO IT AGAIN?   YES ♡   NO ♡

MY BUCKET LIST

#24

_____
_____

WHO/WHAT INSPIRED ME? _____

NEED THIS BECAUSE? _____
_____

TO DO THIS I NEED? _____
_____

I DID IT

DATE COMPLETED _____
LOCATION _____
DETAILS _____
_____
_____
_____

WHAT I LEARNED _____
_____
_____
_____

BEST PART _____
_____
_____

WOULD DO IT AGAIN?   YES   NO

MY BUCKET LIST

#25

_____

_____

WHO/WHAT INSPIRED ME? _____

I NEED THIS BECAUSE? _____

_____

TO DO THIS I NEED? _____

_____

I DID IT

DATE COMPLETED _____

LOCATION _____

DETAILS _____

_____

_____

_____

_____

WHAT I LEARNED _____

_____

_____

BEST PART _____

_____

_____

WOULD DO IT AGAIN?   YES ♡   NO

MY BUCKET LIST

#26

WHO/WHAT INSPIRED ME? _____

I NEED THIS BECAUSE? _____

TO DO THIS I NEED? _____

I DID IT

DATE COMPLETED _____

LOCATION _____

DETAILS _____

WHAT I LEARNED _____

BEST PART _____

WOULD DO IT AGAIN?   YES ♡   NO ♡

MY BUCKET LIST

#27

_____

_____

WHO/WHAT INSPIRED ME? _____

I NEED THIS BECAUSE? _____

_____

TO DO THIS I NEED? _____

_____

I DID IT

DATE COMPLETED _____

LOCATION _____

DETAILS _____

_____

_____

_____

_____

WHAT I LEARNED _____

_____

_____

BEST PART _____

_____

_____

WOULD DO IT AGAIN?   YES ♡   NO ♡

MY BUCKET LIST

#28

_____

_____

WHO/WHAT INSPIRED ME? _____

NEED THIS BECAUSE? _____

O DO THIS I NEED? _____

_____

I DID IT

ATE COMPLETED _____
OCATION _____
ETAILS _____

_____
_____
_____
_____

HAT I LEARNED _____

_____
_____
_____

EST PART _____

_____
_____

VOULD DO IT AGAIN? YES NO

MY BUCKET LIST

#29

_____

_____

WHO/WHAT INSPIRED ME? _____

I NEED THIS BECAUSE? _____

_____

TO DO THIS I NEED? _____

_____

I DID IT

DATE COMPLETED _____

LOCATION _____

DETAILS _____

_____

_____

_____

_____

WHAT I LEARNED _____

_____

_____

_____

BEST PART _____

_____

_____

WOULD DO IT AGAIN?   YES ♡   NO ♡

MY BUCKET LIST

#30

_____
_____

WHO/WHAT INSPIRED ME? _____

NEED THIS BECAUSE? _____
_____

TO DO THIS I NEED? _____
_____

I DID IT

DATE COMPLETED _____
LOCATION _____
DETAILS _____
_____
_____
_____
_____

WHAT I LEARNED _____
_____
_____

BEST PART _____
_____
_____

WOULD DO IT AGAIN?   YES ♡   NO ♡

MY BUCKET LIST

#31

_____
_____

WHO/WHAT INSPIRED ME? _____

I NEED THIS BECAUSE? _____
_____

TO DO THIS I NEED? _____
_____

I DID IT

DATE COMPLETED _____
LOCATION _____
DETAILS _____
_____
_____
_____
_____

WHAT I LEARNED _____
_____
_____

BEST PART _____
_____
_____

WOULD DO IT AGAIN?　　YES ♡　　NO ♡

MY BUCKET LIST

_____

_____

#32

WHO/WHAT INSPIRED ME? _____

I NEED THIS BECAUSE? _____

_____

TO DO THIS I NEED? _____

_____

I DID IT

DATE COMPLETED _____

LOCATION _____

DETAILS _____

_____

_____

_____

_____

WHAT I LEARNED _____

_____

_____

BEST PART _____

_____

_____

WOULD DO IT AGAIN?   YES   NO

MY BUCKET LIST

#33

_____

_____

WHO/WHAT INSPIRED ME? _____

I NEED THIS BECAUSE? _____

_____

TO DO THIS I NEED? _____

_____

I DID IT

DATE COMPLETED _____

LOCATION _____

DETAILS _____

_____

_____

_____

_____

WHAT I LEARNED _____

_____

_____

BEST PART _____

_____

_____

WOULD DO IT AGAIN?   YES   NO ♡

MY BUCKET LIST

#34

_____

_____

WHO/WHAT INSPIRED ME? _____

NEED THIS BECAUSE? _____

_____

O DO THIS I NEED? _____

_____

I DID IT

DATE COMPLETED _____

LOCATION _____

DETAILS _____

_____

_____

_____

_____

WHAT I LEARNED _____

_____

_____

_____

BEST PART _____

_____

_____

WOULD DO IT AGAIN?   YES   NO

MY BUCKET LIST

#35

_____

_____

WHO/WHAT INSPIRED ME? _____

I NEED THIS BECAUSE? _____

_____

TO DO THIS I NEED? _____

_____

I DID IT

DATE COMPLETED _____

LOCATION _____

DETAILS _____

_____

_____

_____

_____

WHAT I LEARNED _____

_____

_____

BEST PART _____

_____

_____

WOULD DO IT AGAIN?   YES   NO

MY BUCKET LIST

#36

_____

_____

WHO/WHAT INSPIRED ME? _____

NEED THIS BECAUSE? _____
_____

O DO THIS I NEED? _____
_____

I DID IT

ATE COMPLETED _____
OCATION _____
ETAILS _____
_____
_____
_____
_____

HAT I LEARNED _____
_____
_____
_____

EST PART _____
_____
_____

VOULD DO IT AGAIN?   YES   NO

MY BUCKET LIST

#37

_____

_____

WHO/WHAT INSPIRED ME? _____

I NEED THIS BECAUSE? _____

_____

TO DO THIS I NEED? _____

_____

I DID IT

DATE COMPLETED _____

LOCATION _____

DETAILS _____

_____

_____

_____

_____

WHAT I LEARNED _____

_____

_____

BEST PART _____

_____

_____

WOULD DO IT AGAIN?   YES ♡   NO ♡

MY BUCKET LIST

#38

_____

_____

WHO/WHAT INSPIRED ME? _____

I NEED THIS BECAUSE? _____

TO DO THIS I NEED? _____

I DID IT

DATE COMPLETED _____
LOCATION _____
DETAILS _____

_____

_____

_____

WHAT I LEARNED _____

_____

_____

BEST PART _____

_____

_____

WOULD DO IT AGAIN?   YES   NO

MY BUCKET LIST

#39

_____

_____

WHO/WHAT INSPIRED ME? _____

I NEED THIS BECAUSE? _____
_____

TO DO THIS I NEED? _____
_____

I DID IT

DATE COMPLETED _____
LOCATION _____
DETAILS _____
_____
_____
_____
_____

WHAT I LEARNED _____
_____
_____

BEST PART _____
_____
_____

WOULD DO IT AGAIN?   YES ♡   NO ♡

MY BUCKET LIST

#40

_____

_____

WHO/WHAT INSPIRED ME? _____

NEED THIS BECAUSE? _____

TO DO THIS I NEED? _____

I DID IT

DATE COMPLETED _____
LOCATION _____
DETAILS _____

_____

_____

_____

WHAT I LEARNED _____

_____

_____

BEST PART _____

_____

_____

WOULD DO IT AGAIN?   YES ♡   NO ♡

MY BUCKET LIST

#41

_____

_____

WHO/WHAT INSPIRED ME? _____

I NEED THIS BECAUSE? _____

TO DO THIS I NEED? _____

_____

I DID IT

DATE COMPLETED _____

LOCATION _____

DETAILS _____

_____

_____

_____

_____

WHAT I LEARNED _____

_____

_____

BEST PART _____

_____

_____

WOULD DO IT AGAIN? YES ♡ NO ♡

MY BUCKET LIST

#42

_____

_____

WHO/WHAT INSPIRED ME? _____

NEED THIS BECAUSE? _____

O DO THIS I NEED? _____

I DID IT

ATE COMPLETED _____

OCATION _____

ETAILS _____

_____

_____

_____

WHAT I LEARNED _____

_____

_____

EST PART _____

_____

_____

WOULD DO IT AGAIN?   YES ♡   NO ♡

MY BUCKET LIST

#43

_____

_____

WHO/WHAT INSPIRED ME? _____

I NEED THIS BECAUSE? _____

_____

TO DO THIS I NEED? _____

_____

I DID IT

DATE COMPLETED _____

LOCATION _____

DETAILS _____

_____

_____

_____

_____

WHAT I LEARNED _____

_____

_____

BEST PART _____

_____

_____

WOULD DO IT AGAIN? YES ♡ NO

MY BUCKET LIST

#44

_____

_____

WHO/WHAT INSPIRED ME? _____

I NEED THIS BECAUSE? _____

TO DO THIS I NEED? _____

I DID IT

DATE COMPLETED _____

LOCATION _____

DETAILS _____

_____

_____

_____

_____

WHAT I LEARNED _____

_____

_____

_____

BEST PART _____

_____

_____

WOULD DO IT AGAIN?   YES   NO

MY BUCKET LIST

#45

_____

_____

WHO/WHAT INSPIRED ME? _____

I NEED THIS BECAUSE? _____

_____

TO DO THIS I NEED? _____

_____

I DID IT

DATE COMPLETED _____

LOCATION _____

DETAILS _____

_____

_____

_____

_____

WHAT I LEARNED _____

_____

_____

BEST PART _____

_____

_____

WOULD DO IT AGAIN?   YES   NO

MY BUCKET LIST

_____

_____ **#46**

/HO/WHAT INSPIRED ME? _____

NEED THIS BECAUSE? _____
_____

O DO THIS I NEED? _____
_____

I DID IT

ATE COMPLETED _____
OCATION _____
ETAILS _____
_____
_____
_____
_____

HAT I LEARNED _____
_____
_____
_____

ST PART _____
_____
_____

VOULD DO IT AGAIN?   YES   NO

MY BUCKET LIST

#47

_____
_____

WHO/WHAT INSPIRED ME? _____

I NEED THIS BECAUSE? _____
_____

TO DO THIS I NEED? _____
_____

I DID IT

DATE COMPLETED _____
LOCATION _____
DETAILS _____
_____
_____
_____
_____

WHAT I LEARNED _____
_____
_____

BEST PART _____
_____
_____

WOULD DO IT AGAIN?   YES ♡   NO ♡

MY BUCKET LIST

#48

_____

_____

WHO/WHAT INSPIRED ME? _____

NEED THIS BECAUSE? _____

O DO THIS I NEED? _____

_____

I DID IT

ATE COMPLETED _____
OCATION _____
ETAILS _____

_____

_____

_____

_____

HAT I LEARNED _____

_____

_____

EST PART _____

_____

_____

VOULD DO IT AGAIN?   YES   NO

MY BUCKET LIST

#49

_____

_____

WHO/WHAT INSPIRED ME? _____

I NEED THIS BECAUSE? _____

_____

TO DO THIS I NEED? _____

_____

I DID IT

DATE COMPLETED _____

LOCATION _____

DETAILS _____

_____

_____

_____

WHAT I LEARNED _____

_____

_____

BEST PART _____

_____

_____

WOULD DO IT AGAIN?   YES ♡   NO ♡

MY BUCKET LIST

_____

_____ **#50**

WHO/WHAT INSPIRED ME? _____

I NEED THIS BECAUSE? _____

_____

TO DO THIS I NEED? _____

_____

I DID IT

DATE COMPLETED _____

LOCATION _____

DETAILS _____

_____

_____

_____

_____

WHAT I LEARNED _____

_____

_____

_____

BEST PART _____

_____

_____

WOULD DO IT AGAIN?　　YES ♡　　NO ♡

MY BUCKET LIST

#51

_____

_____

WHO/WHAT INSPIRED ME? _____

I NEED THIS BECAUSE? _____

_____

TO DO THIS I NEED? _____

_____

I DID IT

DATE COMPLETED _____

LOCATION _____

DETAILS _____

_____

_____

_____

_____

WHAT I LEARNED _____

_____

_____

BEST PART _____

_____

_____

WOULD DO IT AGAIN?   YES ♡   NO ♡

MY BUCKET LIST

_____

_____

#52

WHO/WHAT INSPIRED ME? _____

I NEED THIS BECAUSE? _____

_____

TO DO THIS I NEED? _____

_____

I DID IT

DATE COMPLETED _____

LOCATION _____

DETAILS _____

_____

_____

_____

_____

WHAT I LEARNED _____

_____

_____

_____

BEST PART _____

_____

_____

WOULD DO IT AGAIN?   YES   NO

MY BUCKET LIST

#53

_____

_____

WHO/WHAT INSPIRED ME? _____

I NEED THIS BECAUSE? _____

_____

TO DO THIS I NEED? _____

_____

I DID IT

DATE COMPLETED _____

LOCATION _____

DETAILS _____

_____

_____

_____

_____

WHAT I LEARNED _____

_____

_____

BEST PART _____

_____

_____

WOULD DO IT AGAIN? YES ♡ NO ♡

MY BUCKET LIST

#54

_____
_____

WHO/WHAT INSPIRED ME? _____

NEED THIS BECAUSE? _____
_____

O DO THIS I NEED? _____
_____

I DID IT

ATE COMPLETED _____
OCATION _____
ETAILS _____
_____
_____
_____
_____

WHAT I LEARNED _____
_____
_____

EST PART _____
_____
_____

WOULD DO IT AGAIN?   YES   NO

MY BUCKET LIST

#55

_____

_____

WHO/WHAT INSPIRED ME? _____

I NEED THIS BECAUSE? _____

_____

TO DO THIS I NEED? _____

_____

I DID IT

DATE COMPLETED _____

LOCATION _____

DETAILS _____

_____

_____

_____

_____

WHAT I LEARNED _____

_____

_____

BEST PART _____

_____

_____

WOULD DO IT AGAIN?   YES   NO

MY BUCKET LIST

#56

_____

_____

WHO/WHAT INSPIRED ME? _____

I NEED THIS BECAUSE? _____
_____

TO DO THIS I NEED? _____
_____

I DID IT

DATE COMPLETED _____
LOCATION _____
DETAILS _____
_____
_____
_____
_____

WHAT I LEARNED _____
_____
_____

BEST PART _____
_____
_____

WOULD DO IT AGAIN?   YES ♡   NO ♡

MY BUCKET LIST

#57

_____

_____

WHO/WHAT INSPIRED ME? _____

I NEED THIS BECAUSE? _____

_____

TO DO THIS I NEED? _____

_____

I DID IT

DATE COMPLETED _____

LOCATION _____

DETAILS _____

_____

_____

_____

_____

WHAT I LEARNED _____

_____

_____

BEST PART _____

_____

_____

WOULD DO IT AGAIN?   YES   NO

MY BUCKET LIST

#58

_____
_____

WHO/WHAT INSPIRED ME? _____

NEED THIS BECAUSE? _____

TO DO THIS I NEED? _____
_____

I DID IT

DATE COMPLETED _____
LOCATION _____
DETAILS _____
_____
_____
_____
_____

WHAT I LEARNED _____
_____
_____

BEST PART _____
_____
_____

WOULD DO IT AGAIN?   YES   NO

MY BUCKET LIST

#59

_____
_____

WHO/WHAT INSPIRED ME? _____

I NEED THIS BECAUSE? _____
_____

TO DO THIS I NEED? _____
_____

I DID IT

DATE COMPLETED _____
LOCATION _____
DETAILS _____
_____
_____
_____
_____

WHAT I LEARNED _____
_____
_____

BEST PART _____
_____
_____

WOULD DO IT AGAIN? YES ♡ NO ♡

MY BUCKET LIST

#60

_____

_____

WHO/WHAT INSPIRED ME? _____

NEED THIS BECAUSE? _____
_____

O DO THIS I NEED? _____
_____

I DID IT

ATE COMPLETED _____
OCATION _____
ETAILS _____
_____
_____
_____
_____

HAT I LEARNED _____
_____
_____
_____

EST PART _____
_____
_____

WOULD DO IT AGAIN?   YES   NO

MY BUCKET LIST

#61

_____

_____

WHO/WHAT INSPIRED ME? _____

I NEED THIS BECAUSE? _____

_____

TO DO THIS I NEED? _____

_____

I DID IT

DATE COMPLETED _____

LOCATION _____

DETAILS _____

_____

_____

_____

_____

WHAT I LEARNED _____

_____

_____

BEST PART _____

_____

_____

WOULD DO IT AGAIN?   YES   NO

MY BUCKET LIST

#62

_____
_____

WHO/WHAT INSPIRED ME? _____

I NEED THIS BECAUSE? _____
_____

TO DO THIS I NEED? _____
_____

I DID IT

DATE COMPLETED _____
LOCATION _____
DETAILS _____
_____
_____
_____
_____

WHAT I LEARNED _____
_____
_____
_____

BEST PART _____
_____
_____

WOULD DO IT AGAIN? YES NO

MY BUCKET LIST

#63

_____

_____

WHO/WHAT INSPIRED ME? _____

I NEED THIS BECAUSE? _____
_____

TO DO THIS I NEED? _____
_____

I DID IT

DATE COMPLETED _____

LOCATION _____

DETAILS _____
_____
_____
_____
_____

WHAT I LEARNED _____
_____
_____

BEST PART _____
_____
_____

WOULD DO IT AGAIN?   YES ♡   NO ♡

MY BUCKET LIST

_____

_____

#64

WHO/WHAT INSPIRED ME? _____

NEED THIS BECAUSE? _____

O DO THIS I NEED? _____

_____

I DID IT

ATE COMPLETED _____

OCATION _____

ETAILS _____

_____

_____

_____

_____

HAT I LEARNED _____

_____

_____

_____

EST PART _____

_____

_____

VOULD DO IT AGAIN? YES ♡ NO ♡

MY BUCKET LIST

#65

_____

_____

WHO/WHAT INSPIRED ME? _____

I NEED THIS BECAUSE? _____

_____

TO DO THIS I NEED? _____

_____

I DID IT

DATE COMPLETED _____

LOCATION _____

DETAILS _____

_____

_____

_____

_____

WHAT I LEARNED _____

_____

_____

BEST PART _____

_____

_____

WOULD DO IT AGAIN?   YES ♡   NO ♡

MY BUCKET LIST

#66

_____

_____

WHO/WHAT INSPIRED ME? _____

NEED THIS BECAUSE? _____

_____

O DO THIS I NEED? _____

_____

I DID IT

ATE COMPLETED _____

OCATION _____

ETAILS _____

_____

_____

_____

_____

HAT I LEARNED _____

_____

_____

_____

ST PART _____

_____

_____

VOULD DO IT AGAIN?   YES   NO

MY BUCKET LIST

#67

_____

_____

WHO/WHAT INSPIRED ME? _____

I NEED THIS BECAUSE? _____

_____

TO DO THIS I NEED? _____

_____

I DID IT

DATE COMPLETED _____

LOCATION _____

DETAILS _____

_____

_____

_____

_____

WHAT I LEARNED _____

_____

_____

BEST PART _____

_____

_____

WOULD DO IT AGAIN?   YES ♡   NO ♡

MY BUCKET LIST

#68

_____

_____

WHO/WHAT INSPIRED ME? _____

I NEED THIS BECAUSE? _____

TO DO THIS I NEED? _____

I DID IT

DATE COMPLETED _____

LOCATION _____

DETAILS _____

_____

_____

_____

_____

WHAT I LEARNED _____

_____

_____

_____

BEST PART _____

_____

_____

WOULD DO IT AGAIN?   YES   NO

MY BUCKET LIST

#69

_____

_____

WHO/WHAT INSPIRED ME? _____

I NEED THIS BECAUSE? _____

_____

TO DO THIS I NEED? _____

_____

I DID IT

DATE COMPLETED _____

LOCATION _____

DETAILS _____

_____

_____

_____

_____

WHAT I LEARNED _____

_____

_____

BEST PART _____

_____

_____

WOULD DO IT AGAIN?   YES ♡   NO ♡

MY BUCKET LIST

#70

_____

_____

WHO/WHAT INSPIRED ME? _____

NEED THIS BECAUSE? _____

O DO THIS I NEED? _____

_____

I DID IT

ATE COMPLETED _____

OCATION _____

ETAILS _____

_____

_____

_____

_____

HAT I LEARNED _____

_____

_____

_____

EST PART _____

_____

_____

WOULD DO IT AGAIN?   YES ♡   NO ♡

NOTES

NOTES

NOTES

NOTES

NOTES

_____

_____

_____

_____

_____

_____

_____

_____

_____

_____

_____

_____

_____

_____

_____

NOTES

NOTES

NOTES

NOTES

NOTES

NOTES

_____

_____

_____

_____

_____

_____

_____

_____

_____

_____

_____

_____

_____

_____

_____

_____

NOTES

NOTES

Printed in Great Britain
by Amazon

19175691R00058